LIFE'S GRE

DESTRUCTI

The Omnibus

A Parody

Charles Sherwood Dane

WARNER BOOKS

A *Warner* Book

First published in this omnibus edition in Great Britain in 1997 by Warner Books
This omnibus edition copyright © 1997 The Stonesong Press, Inc.

LIFE'S LITTLE DESTRUCTION BOOK first published in the United States in 1992
by St. Martin's Press
First published in Great Britain in 1993 by Warner Books
Copyright © 1992 The Stonesong Press, Inc.

MORE LIFE'S LITTLE DESTRUCTION BOOK first published in the United States in 1993
by St. Martin's Press
First published in Great Britain in 1994 by Warner Books
Copyright © 1993 The Stonesong Press, Inc.

The moral right of the author has been asserted.

A CIP catalogue record for this book is available from the British Library.

ISBN 0 7515 2234 1

Photoset in North Wales by Derek Doyle & Associates, Mold, Flintshire.
Printed and bound in Great Britain by
Clays Ltd, St Ives plc

Warner Books
A Division of
Little, Brown and Company (UK)
Brettenham House
Lancaster Place
London WC2E 7EN

INTRODUCTION

Goody two-shoeism hangs like an angel's halo over the land, pressuring us to improve ourselves and constantly do the right thing. Recycling has us going around in circles. Sensitivity shades into silliness. One more rant about co-dependency and we will all go cuckoo. There are just too many good things to do.

Unchecked, the pursuit of perfection threatens to erase the little quirks and foibles and peculiarities that make us *us*. If we become any nicer, better behaved, more socially concerned, blissful – or repressed – we could end up a nation of axe murderers.

Enough already. The prescriptions and advice in these pages are meant as an antidote to niceness run rampant. The book points the way back towards sanity. Let each sentence be your clarion call. Think small and indulge yourself; vent your spleen lest it explode and splatter your neighbour. Go ahead and be a little obnoxious: make sucking noises; be pushy. Learn again to belittle, belabour and betray. Use more plastic, grind your teeth and experience again the exquisite satisfaction you once knew as a child when you peed in the pool. The future of Western civilization may depend on it.

And maybe we've softened but in this bumper edition there are two additional bonuses for you:

1) Little White Lies you can tell to cover your you know what, and

2) A bunch of ways to make yourself totally miserable. We call these Self Destructions.

Now go out there and make us proud!

Along with goodness, there is all too much gratitude in this society, but grudging thanks still must go to the following for their contributions: Ned Bienemann, Gene Brown, Sheree Bykofsky, Bob Detmer, David Dinin, Christopher Fargis, Paul Fargis, Victoria Gallucci, Gail Girardet, Caroline McKeldin, Adam O'Conner, Lea Bayers Rapp, Tricia Reinus, Celine Texier Rose, Dawn Sangrey, Wendy Silbert, Lynne Ward, and Jennifer Weis.

1 ◆ Never tip more than ten pence.

2 ◆ Keep the chain letters going.

3 ◆ Post-date all your cheques.

4 ◆ Hum along at the concert.

5 ◆ Take the hotel towel.

6 ◆ Signal left; turn right.

7 ◆ Help fools part with their money.

8 ◆ Don't keep secrets.

9 ◆ Pass on the vicious rumours.

10 ◆ Exaggerate on your CV.

11 ◆ Let everyone know how hard you work.

12 ◆ Practise the art of limp handshakes.

13 ◆ Hire yourself a devious accountant; it's like giving yourself a raise.

14 ◆ Buy this book.

15 ◆ Read other people's mail.

16 ◆ Pay bus fares with £20 notes.

17 ◆ If the mistake is in your favour, don't correct it.

18 ◆ Butter up the boss.

19 ◆ Talk with your hand over your mouth.

20 ◆ Misquote.

21 ◆ Tell the ending of movies.

22 ◆ Use sexist innuendos to get more attention.

23 ◆ Stand up your date.

24 ◆ Give little kids clothes for their birthdays.

25 ◆ Fire people by phone.

26 ◆ Sniff a lot

27 ◆ Never make your bed.

28 ◆ Cut people off in the middle of their sentences.

29 ◆ Slouch.

30 ◆ Wear jeans to weddings.

31 ◆ Leave the toilet seat up.

32 ◆ Add insult to injury.

33 ◆ Drive at 50 mph in the fast lane.

34 ◆ Park in the disabled space.

35 ◆ Pay by cheque at the cash-only till.

36 ◆ Fumble for change when boarding buses.

37 ◆ Borrow a book and dog-ear the pages.

38 ◆ Put your lights on full beam for oncoming traffic.

39 ◆ Finish other people's crossword puzzles.

40 ◆ Ask people what they paid for their clothes.

41 ◆ Rake the leaves into your neighbour's garden.

42 ◆ Pinch your spouse's love handles.

43 ◆ Don't sign your cheques.

44 ◆ Mumble.

45 ◆ Develop a convenient memory.

46 ◆ Take personal calls during important meetings.

47 ◆ Take your ghetto blaster to the beach.

48 ◆ Remind people that their freckles could be cancerous.

49 ◆ Don't return phone calls.

50 ◆ Use the last square of toilet paper.

51 ◆ Ask people how much they earn.

52 ◆ Don't flush.

53 ◆ Burn rubber at the green light.

54 ◆ Leave a half-sucked cough drop on the new sofa.

55 ◆ Tailgate the elderly.

56 ◆ Tell your kids to try even harder.

57 ◆ Tear articles from magazines in the doctor's waiting room.

58 ◆ Put sticky jam pots back in the cupboard.

59 ◆ Let the phone keep on ringing.

60 ◆ Don't dot your i's or cross your t's.

61 ◆ Carve your name on park benches.

62 ◆ Leave your thumb prints on photographs.

63 ◆ Hold off paying the bills which don't charge interest.

64 ◆ Send anonymous letters.

65 ◆ Drink from other people's glasses.

66 ◆ Develop a truly tasteless foul mouth.

67 ◆ Drum your fingers during other people's presentations.

68 ◆ Leave the concert during the solo or before the applause starts.

69 ◆ Leave the price tags on presents.

70 ◆ Name drop.

71 ◆ Blow out other people's birthday candles.

72 ◆ Don't refill the ice-cube tray.

73 ◆ Leave dairy products open in the refrigerator.

74 ◆ Don't leave a message at the beep.

75 ◆ Talk with your finger in people's faces.

76 ◆ Sleep until noon every day.

77 ◆ Smoke in bed.

78 ◆ Dress 15 years younger.

79 ◆ Forget to wash in the morning.

80 ◆ Be a day late for your anniversary.

81 ◆ Always be right.

82 ◆ Lean on the doorbell.

83 ◆ If there is going to be a fight, make sure you start it.

84 ◆ Don't take "no" for an answer.

85 ◆ Ignore "No Smoking" signs.

86 ◆ Bark orders.

87 ◆ Put coal in Christmas stockings.

88 ◆ Sneer at people who try hard.

89 ◆ Assume everybody agrees with you, but keep trying to convince them.

90 ◆ Brag a lot.

91 ◆ Leave your supermarket trolley on the street or in the car park.

92 ◆ Pledge money that you won't be sending.

93 ◆ Leave desk drawers and filing cabinets open.

94 ◆ Don't vote.

95 ◆ Wash whites with coloureds.

96 ◆ Use gift wrapping paper a second time.

97 ◆ Crack your knuckles.

98 ◆ Follow the letter of the law, not the spirit.

99 ◆ Reserve compliments for people who can do you some good.

100 ◆ Treat underlings as such.

101 ◆ Argue with everybody.

102 ◆ Touch the paintings in the gallery.

103 ◆ Get hysterical.

104 ◆ Block the entrances of lifts, buses and the Underground.

105 ◆ Insinuate, implicate and insist.

106 ◆ Threaten legal action.

107 ◆ Pass the buck.

108 ◆ Eat fruit at the greengrocer; don't buy it.

109 ◆ Flaunt it.

110 ◆ Toss trousers with tissues in the pockets into the washing machine.

111 ◆ Prevaricate, obfuscate and complicate.

112 ◆ Remember that your teenager is still a child when buying tickets or paying fares.

113 ◆ Use only American spelling and punctuation.

114 ◆ Gamble with the rent money.

115 ◆ Record over a borrowed videotape.

116 ◆ Tell people they are in your will even if they aren't.

117 ◆ Nurture conspiracy theories.

118 ◆ Don't get caught.

119 ◆ Ask for a rush job except when there is a charge.

120 ◆ Stay directly in front of or behind fire engines and ambulances.

121 ◆ Don't cross until the amber light starts flashing.

122 ◆ When giving directions, leave out a turn or two.

123 ◆ Dream up special requests for waiters and waitresses.

124 ◆ Every umbrella is yours.

125 ◆ Pry.

126 ◆ Don't make up your mind.

127 ◆ Practise passive aggression.

128 ◆ Toss things out of the car window: tissues, cigarettes, sweet wrappers and those sorts of little things.

129 ◆ Try whining.

130 ◆ Improve your posture by walking with your nose in the air.

131 ◆ Remind people who lose their job that they probably should have worked harder.

132 ◆ Accuse, confuse and refuse.

133 ◆ Prophesy woe, financial chaos and domination by Germany.

134 ◆ Leave the Christmas decorations up until March or April.

135 ◆ Talk with your mouth full.

136 ◆ Comment on weight gain in others.

137 ◆ Ask her if the diamond ring is real.

138 ◆ Keep a store of wisecracks for tense and serious occasions.

139 ◆ Pound the table.

140 ◆ Try the expert trail the day you first put on skis.

141 ◆ Scratch your spots whenever you want.

142 ◆ If it feels good, do it.

143 ◆ Answer a question with a question.

144 ◆ See what it takes to get a fellow passenger to pull the communication cord.

145 ◆ Serve corn on the cob to people with dentures.

146 ◆ Don't give to charities unless you get something back.

147 ◆ If you have to give blood, at least make a big show of it.

148 ◆ Have your secretary do all your personal shopping.

149 ◆ Ask the air stewardess a question every five minutes or so.

150 ◆ Assume that your place is next to the hostess.

151 ◆ Add the straw that breaks the camel's back.

152 ◆ Clean your fingernails at the dinner table.

153 ◆ Take but don't pass on phone messages.

154 ◆ Stopping for red lights after midnight is a waste of precious time.

155 ◆ Tuck a twenty-pound note or two in with your driving licence so the traffic cop will take the hint.

156 ◆ Tell people what you think they want to hear.

157 ◆ Notice good ideas and pass them off as your own.

158 ◆ Smuggle a little.

159 ◆ Put the gals in the office in charge of the coffee.

160 ◆ Make jokes about terrorists at the boarding gate.

161 ◆ See if you can be the first one off the plane even if you are sitting by the window.

162 ◆ Put a title like Lord or Doctor before your name when making dinner and hotel reservations.

163 ◆ Balance your bank account every six months or so.

164 ◆ Have an alias and the IDs to prove it.

165 ◆ Keep two sets of books.

166 ◆ Don't volunteer for the back seat and never take the middle one.

167 ◆ Leave town.

168 ◆ Leave the lights on.

169 ◆ Before leaving the lift, push all the buttons.

170 ◆ Give unsolicited advice.

171 ◆ Don't do anything until you have been asked twice.

172 ◆ Put off until tomorrow whatever you can do the day after tomorrow.

173 ◆ Spot test "Wet Paint" signs.

174 ◆ Say "you know" at the end of sentences, you know?

175 ◆ Don't shower after exercising.

176 ◆ Go up the down escalator.

177 ◆ Develop at least three strategies for cutting into the front of queues.

178 ◆ Change channels without asking.

179 ◆ Underline in other people's books.

180 ◆ Goose the bride and the groom.

181 ◆ Call the wife "the little woman".

182 ◆ Lie about your age.

183 ◆ Tell people what you expect them to give you for your birthday.

184 ◆ If you can't think of something nice, say something nasty.

185 ◆ Slurp your soup.

186 ◆ Be judgmental.

187 ◆ Snap your chewing gum.

188 ◆ Focus on winning and to Hell with how you play the game.

189 ◆ Squeeze the toothpaste from the top and, while you're at it, leave the cap off.

190 ◆ Free cable TV is only a shady electrician away.

191 ◆ Send smutty cards to your in-laws.

192 ◆ Open umbrellas in crowded corridors.

193 ◆ Announce when you're going to the toilet.

194 ◆ Read over people's shoulders on the bus.

195 ◆ Hold out until the other man gives in.

196 ◆ Ignore deadlines.

197 ◆ Revenge is sweet; get some.

198 ◆ Borrow money from your mother-in-law.

199 ◆ When it says "Reserved Parking", that means you.

200 ◆ Pad your expense account.

201 ◆ Take the labels off unopened cans.

202 ◆ Adjust your underwear in public.

203 ◆ Cover up your mistakes and pass on the blame.

204 ◆ Borrow handkerchiefs to blow your nose.

205 ◆ Eat all the chocolates until you find the one you want.

206 ◆ Curse the referee at the under-elevens football match.

207 ◆ When you're done with your gum, stick it under the chair.

208 ◆ If you do something nice, make sure everyone knows about it.

209 ◆ Bribe kids; they are easy.

210 ◆ Needle, meddle, coddle, diddle, fiddle.

211 ◆ Gatecrash private meetings with a big smile on your face.

212 ◆ Read the paper during family meals.

213 ◆ Be a perfectionist in absolutely everything.

214 ◆ Put an obscene message on your answerphone.

215 ◆ Be ambiguous; it lets you work both sides of the issue.

216 ◆ Measure people by the money they have and the clothes they wear.

217 ◆ Leave your tights hanging in the bathroom.

218 ◆ Dish out the dirt, but don't take it.

219 ◆ Chew other people's pencils.

220 ◆ Support the death penalty for parking violations.

221 ◆ Get a backseat driver's licence.

222 ◆ Apologize a lot but don't change.

223 ◆ Change the rules to suit your needs.

224 ◆ Lie to your therapist and sit in her chair.

225 ◆ Put your cigarettes out in plant pots.

226 ◆ Make your children stand at attention
every morning.

227 ◆ Wear T-shirts with gross messages.

228 ◆ Leave your shopping trolley in the queue at the checkout – then go shopping.

229 ◆ Pull the covers over to your side.

230 ◆ Leave wet towels on the bedspread.

231 ◆ Let doors slam behind you – in people's faces.

232 ◆ Cut your toe-nails in bed.

233 ◆ Repeat yourself.

234 ◆ Repeat yourself.

235 ◆ Quote Adolf Hitler.

236 ◆ Don't know when to stop.

237 ◆ Tell teenagers how things were in your day.

238 ◆ Play office politics.

239 ◆ Vividly describe a hysterectomy when the entrée arrives.

240 ◆ Put things back where they don't belong.

241 ◆ Use the whole can of starter fluid on the barbecue.

242 ◆ Hold the lift until you have finished your conversation.

243 ◆ Scrawl your signature on important documents.

244 ◆ Take your colicky baby to the cinema.

245 ◆ Hand out your business cards at funerals.

246 ◆ Have belching contests in restaurants.

247 ◆ Clean your ear with your little finger.

248 ◆ Let your blind date know she isn't up to
what you were told.

249 ◆ Make the same mistake twice.

250 ◆ Pee in the swimming pool.

251 ◆ Drive on the hard shoulder until you pass the tailback; then cut in.

252 ◆ Master and practise your best wolf whistle.

253 ◆ Wear large hats during the movies.

254 ◆ Wear golf shoes on newly polished wooden floors.

255 ◆ Chew ice cubes.

256 ◆ Leave wire hangers on the wardrobe floor.

257 ◆ Always have an ulterior motive.

258 ◆ Push the panic button every other day.

259 ◆ Take the biggest piece.

260 ◆ Expectorate on the pavement.

261 ◆ Walk your pit bull without a lead.

262 ◆ Forget the pooper scooper.

263 ◆ Get up on the wrong side of the bed.

264 ◆ Forget the punchline, but don't let that stop you from telling jokes.

265 ◆ Grumble constantly.

266 ◆ Race the old woman for the last bus seat.

267 ◆ Take cheap shots.

268 ◆ Comb your hair in the kitchen.

269 ◆ Take forever to find your word in Scrabble ®.

270 ◆ Cause gridlock.

271 ♦ Remember that everything was better years ago.

272 ♦ Bring 8 changes of clothing to the gym.

273 ♦ Have net practice near the greenhouse.

274 ♦ Change your mind.

275 ♦ Glue a chip to your shoulder.

276 ♦ Blame the victim.

277 ♦ Put salt in the sugar containers.

278 ◆ Greet each new day with a growl.

279 ◆ Put your initials in wet concrete.

280 ◆ Crack the spines of good books.

281 ◆ Draw moustaches on posters.

282 ◆ Don't rewind videocassettes before bringing them back.

283 ◆ Dangle participles.

284 ◆ Exercise chutzpah.

285 ◆ Whistle a happy tune – over and over again.

286 ◆ Walk tall, carry a big stick, and use it.

287 ◆ Give out other people's ex-directory phone numbers.

288 ◆ Take money from your child's piggy bank.

289 ◆ Install a siren in your car.

290 ◆ Serve turkey burgers, British sherry and semolina pud for Christmas.

291 ◆ Do unto others as you would never have them do unto you.

292 ◆ Have a penny, take a penny.

293 ◆ Be vague.

294 ◆ Grab someone else's taxi.

295 ◆ Walk very slowly, and make sure nobody can get past you.

296 ◆ Assign names to your body parts, like "winkie".

297 ◆ Put advertisements under people's windscreen wipers.

298 ◆ When others are in a hurry, take your time.

299 ◆ Use a lawn sprinkler during a hosepipe ban.

300 ◆ Chase ambulances.

301 ◆ Overstay your welcome.

302 ◆ Hedge and waffle.

303 ◆ Kick sand at the beach.

304 ◆ Serve fish with the head still on.

305 ◆ Touch strangers.

306 ◆ Guilt trip.

307 ◆ Fog up the bathroom mirror.

308 ◆ Tell how awfully big your haemorrhoids are.

309 ◆ Tell little children the truth about Santa Claus.

310 ◆ Hit below the belt.

311 ◆ Bite your dentist's finger.

312 ◆ He who has the gold rules.

313 ◆ Remember the Sabbath and sleep late.

314 ◆ Worry your mother.

315 ◆ Pick your scabs.

316 ◆ Change horses in midstream.

317 ◆ Let the crumbs fall on the floor, and the chips where they may.

318 ◆ Get up early and take your neighbour's newspaper.

319 ◆ Drive like a cabbie.

320 ◆ Point out mispronunciations.

321 ◆ Sneeze in a crowded lift.

322 ◆ Get into a heated argument about the weather.

323 ◆ Please feed the animals in the zoo.

324 ◆ Spring back; fall ahead.

325 ◆ Open the coffin for one last look.

326 ◆ Leave the alarm on when he doesn't have to get up.

327 ◆ Shake up the fizzy drinks before opening them.

328 ◆ Make animal noises in libraries.

329 ◆ Fart in cramped public spaces.

330 ◆ Never forgive nor forget.

331 ◆ Don't tell the committee that you cancelled the meeting.

332 ◆ Ask people how they are, but don't wait for a response.

333 ◆ Cut somebody today, but only if it's undeserved.

334 ◆ Fish on private property.

335 ◆ Leave lipstick prints on people's cheeks and foreheads.

336 ◆ Assume the authority but not the responsibility.

337 ◆ Get your back up.

338 ◆ Think nothing of it.

339 ◆ Appease belligerents.

340 ◆ Don't stand during hymns and anthems.

341 ◆ Be generous with backhanded compliments.

342 ◆ Try looking down your nose at newcomers.

343 ◆ Find good things to say about Robert Maxwell.

344 ◆ Don't put stamps on your letters.

345 ◆ Swear 'til you're blue in the face.

346 ◆ Wait five weeks to deposit cheques.

347 ◆ Borrow your flatmate's diaphragm.

348 ◆ Live in a glass house and throw stones.

349 ◆ Procrastinate and someone else will surely do it.

350 ◆ Eat like a horse and make a pig of yourself.

351 ◆ Drown your sorrows by bending the elbow.

352 ◆ If you can do the time, do the crime.

353 ◆ Believe that numbers and stars influence the way your life works.

354 ◆ Use more plastic.

355 ◆ Put all your eggs in one basket.

356 ◆ Play with fire.

357 ◆ Split hairs.

358 ◆ Let slip the dogs of war.

359 ◆ Cut corners.

360 ◆ Drown yourself in perfume.

361 ◆ Never eat crow, hats or humble pie.

362 ◆ Fish for compliments.

363 ◆ Crack the whip.

364 ◆ Have bones to pick.

365 ◆ Dance fast to slow music and vice versa.

366 ◆ Cook everything with chili peppers.

367 ◆ Drink orange juice right out of the carton.

368 ◆ Burn your bridges and candles at both ends.

369 ◆ Call your spouse by the name of an old flame.

370 ◆ Heads you win, tails you win.

371 ◆ Take bulbs from the landing lights when you need them in your flat.

372 ◆ Pass on the left in traffic.

373 ◆ Put pennies in the collection plate.

374 ◆ Lean way back in delicate old chairs.

375 ◆ Make fun of all accents.

376 ◆ Don't sign your greeting cards.

377 ◆ Leave papers in the copier.

378 ◆ Rubberneck.

379 ◆ Neck and pet in public places.

380 ◆ Ask your parents and grandparents how much they plan to leave you.

381 ◆ Brush the dandruff off other people's shoulders.

382 ◆ Lick the knife before putting it back in the strawberry jam.

383 ◆ Suspect a plot.

384 ◆ Tell long, boring stories.

385 ◆ Be "in conference" all the time.

386 ◆ Pinch kids' cheeks.

387 ◆ Bitch, bitch, bitch.

388 ◆ Get into every photograph you can.

389 ◆ Have a "Clergy on Call" sign made for your windscreen.

390 ◆ Slap people on the back.

391 ◆ Swear this time you mean it – really.

392 ◆ Whisper behind their backs.

393 ◆ Misfile everything, especially contracts.

394 ◆ Remind friends of stupid things they did
ten years ago.

395 ◆ Bum cigarettes.

396 ◆ Park in front of driveways and emergency exits.

397 ◆ Don't tear the edges off computer paper.

398 ◆ Let your nose hair grow out.

399 ◆ Don't wash the milk bottles.

400 ◆ Shave every third or fourth day.

401 ◆ Eat crackers in bed, and then move to your side.

402 ◆ Cover your living-room furniture in plastic.

403 ◆ Mix up books on library shelves.

404 ◆ Overtake funeral processions.

405 ◆ Flash your Rolex, even if it's phony.

406 ◆ Tape-record phone conversations and use them later for revenge.

407 ◆ Feed the dog under the table.

408 ◆ Refuse to use the drink mat.

409 ◆ Don't mow the lawn more than once or twice a summer.

410 ◆ Buy it, wear it, return it.

411 ◆ Be unprepared for public appearances.

412 ◆ Ask if a present is returnable.

413 ◆ Overconsume and buy on impulse.

414 ◆ Tell people they have bad breath.

415 ◆ Keep your car moving fast near the pavement puddles.

416 ◆ Call friends during the Cup Final to talk out your problems.

417 ◆ Copy copyrighted software.

418 ◆ Drink hot coffee while driving.

419 ◆ Don't tell vegetarians about the meat in the casserole.

420 ◆ Occupy a café table for hours with one cup of coffee.

421 ◆ Smell smoke often and announce it.

422 ◆ Keep saying, "That's nice."

423 ◆ Wear sheep's clothing.

424 ◆ Open old wounds whenever possible.

425 ◆ Brag about your new fur in a pet shop.

426 ◆ Tell jokes at funerals.

427 ◆ Throw a loud party in the middle of the week.

428 ◆ Convince other people to take risks you wouldn't touch.

429 ◆ Eat out with friends and "forget" your wallet.

430 ◆ Be nothing if not critical.

431 ◆ Practise pulling the wool over people's eyes.

432 ◆ Don't call to cancel reservations.

433 ◆ Sulk.

434 ◆ Be known for your sesquipedalianism.

435 ◆ Quote proverbs in Latin.

436 ◆ Go topless or all the way on public beaches.

437 ◆ Put everyone on the speaker phone.

438 ◆ Play with marked cards.

439 ◆ Develop the skill of cutting people down to size.

440 ◆ Refuse to have a nice day.

441 ◆ Say "uh" after every word.

442 ◆ Write Dear John letters.

443 ◆ Step on the back of the shoe of the person in front of you.

444 ◆ Deception is power.

445 ◆ Alternately raise and lower your voice to make people question their hearing.

446 ◆ Keep asking, "Are we there yet?"

447 ◆ Belittle, belabour and betray.

448 ◆ Declare "just cause" at weddings.

449 ◆ Use up all the hot water.

450 ◆ Beg the questions.

451 ◆ Find the loopholes.

452 ◆ Covet thy neighbour or his wife.

453 ◆ Bet a beggar double or nothing.

454 ◆ Don't knock.

455 ◆ Refuse reverse-charge phone calls from your family.

456 ◆ If you don't get your way, take your ball and bat and go home.

457 ◆ Clean up your boss's desk.

458 ◆ Hog the dryer at the laundrette.

459 ◆ Eat off your date's plate.

460 ◆ Drink your flatmate's last beer.

461 ◆ Shave your legs with your husband's razor.

462 ◆ Use fly spray in the car.

463 ◆ Bite off more than you can chew.

464 ◆ Eat garlic just before business meetings and intimate dinners.

465 ◆ Indulge in character assassination.

466 ◆ Jiggle your foot continuously during job interviews.

467 ◆ Wallow in self-pity.

468 ◆ Never dust.

469 ◆ Make scary faces at babies.

470 ◆ Run amok.

471 ◆ Look over the repairman's shoulder and offer advice.

472 ◆ Put your feet on the table.

473 ◆ Play mind games.

474 ◆ Recommend untrustworthy car mechanics.

475 ◆ Buy and read the *Daily Sport*.

476 ◆ Bite the hand that feeds you.

477 ◆ Open money presents at the wedding and announce the amount.

478 ◆ Tell everyone that they should be in therapy.

479 ◆ Flirt with a friend's spouse.

480 ◆ Lie with statistics.

481 ◆ Say the coffee is decaf when it isn't.

482 ◆ Serve wine in beer mugs or liqueur glasses.

483 ◆ Give distances in kilometres.

484 ◆ Tell a friend who has had a disaster to look on the bright side of it.

485 ◆ Make fun of men who cry.

486 ◆ Leave your fly open.

487 ◆ Throw out the baby with the bath water.

488 ◆ Borrow money from friends and then deny you did.

489 ◆ Put steel-tips on your shoes.

490 ◆ Leave used dental floss on the bathroom basin.

491 ◆ Learn to recognize suckers and sitting ducks.

492 ◆ Don't show up after you offer someone a lift.

493 ◆ Bring a bar of soap to the health-club Jacuzzi.

494 ◆ Disturb the peace.

495 ◆ Stand in the home terraces and cheer for the other team.

496 ◆ Pretend you're listening.

497 ◆ Step on your dance partner's foot.

498 ◆ Don't back up your computer data.

499 ◆ Cast the first stone.

500 ◆ Don't call your mother.

501 ◆ Make sure you win when you play games with kids.

502 ◆ Never acknowledge anyone else's contribution to any thing.

503 ◆ Serve red wine with fish.

504 ◆ Don't date business letters.

505 ◆ Jump to conclusions.

506 ◆ Be a bad sport.

507 ◆ Shake with your left hand.

508 ◆ RSVP on the last possible day.

509 ◆ Answer the phone with, "What do you want?"

510 ◆ Put the fork on the right and the knife on the left.

511 ◆ Put people on hold with a Barry Manilow tape playing.

512 ◆ Have one for the road.

513 ◆ Carry a grudge.

514 ◆ Wait until you're in the voting booth to decide.

515 ◆ Cross your leg over and keep shaking your foot.

516 ◆ Emulate Bart Simpson.

517 ◆ Whatever it is, be against it.

518 ◆ Power Trip.

519 ◆ Be first on the bus, then grope around for change.

520 ◆ Bring an uninvited guest to the wedding.

521 ◆ Make sure the car behind you catches the red light.

522 ◆ Pretend you didn't hear the question.

523 ◆ Before you give that hearty handshake, sneeze into your hand.

524 ◆ Tell kids, "Sleep tight; don't let the bed bugs bite."

525 ◆ When you do something bad, use someone else's name.

526 ◆ When you're in a foreign country, refuse to speak the language.

527 ◆ When the collection plate is passed to you, help yourself.

528 ◆ At a convention, stare at people's badges when you talk to them.

529 ◆ Assign blame.

530 ◆ Raise your voice so that people who don't speak English will understand.

531 ◆ Develop a truly blank look.

532 ◆ Drool.

533 ◆ Get drunk before PTA meetings.

534 ◆ Staple cheque to paying-in slip before posting.

535 ◆ Walk on freshly seeded grass.

536 ◆ Eavesdrop.

537 ◆ Blow your horn as soon as the light turns green.

538 ◆ Blow your stack.

539 ◆ Paint your fingernails on the aeroplane.

540 ◆ Seduce a superior, and then claim sexual harassment.

541 ◆ House an illegal alien.

542 ◆ Turn up the volume on late movies.

543 ◆ Rub everyone up the wrong way.

544 ◆ Actually chill out.

545 ◆ Begin a job interview by asking about the holidays.

546 ◆ Poke kids playfully in their belly-buttons.

547 ◆ Tell your hostess her dishes are dirty.

548 ◆ Brush your hair in the kitchen.

549 ◆ Dampen spirits and edit out joy.

550 ◆ Serve runny eggs.

551 ◆ Use a loudhailer to call the ref obscene names.

552 ◆ Strive to be politically perfect, not just politically correct.

553 ◆ Go to the concert with a hacking cough.

554 ◆ When the pianist pauses, applaud.

555 ◆ Scratch your crotch in public.

556 ◆ Breastfeed your twins at the stadium.

557 ◆ Be one of the guys who just doesn't get it.

558 ◆ Show people where they went wrong.

559 ◆ Stare at the chests of big-breasted women.

560 ◆ Insist you were there first.

561 ◆ Remember, all's fair in love and war.

562 ◆ Convert to humanism in church.

563 ◆ Send gifts C.O.D.

564 ◆ Be redundant, time and time again.

565 ◆ Talk in rhyme all the time.

566 ◆ Never, never change your routine.

567 ◆ Look busy.

568 ◆ Leave lipstick on his collar.

569 ◆ Outline his bald spot with your finger.

570 ◆ If you sprinkle when you tinkle, just leave it.

571 ◆ Pull the rug out from under someone.

572 ◆ Collect Sweet 'n Low from restaurants.

573 ◆ Tell your friend about her surprise party.

574 ◆ Have all the answers.

575 ◆ Suggest to mourners that they cheer up and look on the bright side.

576 ◆ Shuffle someone else's alphabetical file.

577 ◆ Tickle people.

578 ◆ Say you're sorry in a cheerful, lilting voice.

579 ◆ Slap people on the back.

580 ◆ Bite into the piece of fruit before offering it to someone else.

581 ◆ Show up late.

582 ◆ Leave early.

583 ◆ Ride your bike on crowded pavements.

584 ◆ Make notes on linen napkins in restaurants.

585 ◆ Recommend that she shave her legs more often.

586 ◆ Crash your way into a parking space.

587 ◆ Be in contempt of court.

588 ◆ Bear false witness.

589 ◆ "Shoot" the messenger.

590 ◆ Leave your name in wet cement.

591 ◆ Break hearts, wind, and rules.

592 ◆ Bring pizza and beer to the Intensive Care Unit.

593 ◆ Tell your children that babies come from storks.

594 ◆ When you get close to celebrities, rip off a piece of their clothing.

595 ◆ Contradict your spouse loudly in public.

596 ◆ The phonier the better.

597 ◆ Ask very personal questions.

598 ◆ Take advantage of everyone.

599 ◆ Play mind games.

600 ◆ Don't replace the toilet paper roll.

601 ◆ Preach gloom and doom.

602 ◆ Throw your money around.

603 ◆ Leave other people's business cards in telephone boxes.

604 ◆ Give your friends' names to mailing lists and telephone sales people.

605 ◆ Insist that people search for things that aren't lost.

606 ◆ Get one of those "Theme from The Godfather" car horns.

607 ◆ Practise misanthropy and misogyny.

608 ◆ Go ahead even when you know you are making a mistake.

609 ◆ Go to bed angry.

610 ◆ If you can't bedazzle them with your brilliance, baffle them with your bullshit.

611 ◆ Try getting away with murder.

612 ◆ If that doesn't work, try mayhem.

613 ◆ Suggest nose jobs to your friends.

614 ◆ Don't know and don't care.

615 ◆ Lash out at people who are only trying to help.

616 ◆ An ounce of cure is worth a pound of prevention.

617 ◆ Mail the postcards after you get back from vacation.

618 ◆ Delve into things that are none of your business.

619 ◆ Fill out deposit slips at the cashier's window.

620 ◆ See how tall and yellow your lawn can get.

621 ◆ Touch the tip of your shoes against the heels of the person in the queue in front of you.

622 ◆ Create warring factions in your family.

623 ◆ Ask them to name all 54 flavours, then order vanilla.

624 ◆ Believe you are above the law.

625 ◆ Lean back and look at your visitor through a thin, cold smile.

626 ◆ No need to say please or thank you.

627 ◆ Love is never having to say you're sorry.

628 ◆ Moan and groan.

629 ◆ Doubletalk.

630 ◆ Count your chickens before they are conceived.

631 ◆ Play monkey in the middle with your little niece.

632 ◆ Split the bill only when your meal costs more.

633 ◆ When you scratch his back, avoid the spot that itches.

634 ◆ Reserve the sunlounger and then go swimming all day.

635 ◆ Finish people's sentences for them.

636 ◆ Toss and turn when you're sleeping over.

637 ◆ Serve children blue cheese dressing.

638 ◆ You're right. The world does revolve around you.

639 ◆ Put a video camera in the employee washroom.

640 ◆ Make a visitor stand.

641 ◆ Elbow your way through a crowd.

642 ◆ Concentrate on trivia.

643 ◆ Don't hesitate: show the contempt you feel.

644 ◆ Humiliate someone when you need to establish control.

645 ◆ Stop and stare at accidents.

646 ◆ Tell everyone to prove it.

647 ◆ Prop your feet up on the boss's desk.

648 ◆ Borrow receipts to take to the IRS audit.

649 ◆ Slip a foul word by the personal number plate censors.

650 ◆ Weave in and out of traffic just for fun.

651 ◆ Never let it be good enough.

652 ◆ Always play devil's advocate.

653 ◆ Wear a string bikini at
the gym.

654 ◆ Rapidly recite your address to someone who is writing it down.

655 ◆ Stop as soon as you get off the escalator.

656 ◆ Tell your colleague you overheard a plan to fire him.

657 ◆ Leave a note from the tooth fairy, "Out of cash".

658 ◆ Tell him that you bought a false Rolex just like his.

659 ◆ Point out that her necklace emphasises her double chin.

660 ◆ Allow every man his say, then contradict it.

661 ◆ Invite them for dinner and don't be home.

662 ◆ When you're really needed, leave town.

663 ◆ Eat garlic bread before your dental appointment.

664 ◆ Leave the soap on the shower floor.

665 ◆ Pollute.

666 ◆ Lie in confession.

667 ◆ Tell tall tales.

668 ◆ Comment on the contents of your host's bathroom cabinet.

669 ◆ Leave your messes for someone else to clean up.

670 ◆ Recommend an inept financial advisor.

671 ◆ Entertain flight passengers with crash stories.

672 ◆ Toss paper towels in the public toilet.

673 ◆ Adjust the reception while he's watching the big game.

674 ◆ Blow your nose at the dinner table.

675 ◆ Pull lint from his belly-button.

676 ◆ Wipe off your eye make-up on the guest towels.

677 ◆ Tell a sick person about people you know who died.

678 ◆ Squeak chalk across the blackboard.

679 ◆ Tap their glassware to see if it rings.

680 ◆ When you meet people, make it clear you're sizing them up.

681 ◆ Don't come when you're called.

682 ◆ Keep on talking and talking and talking.

683 ◆ Have a cow.

684 ◆ Cheat at snooker.

685 ◆ Always aim low.

686 ◆ Pick your nose and eat it.

687 ◆ When the doctor says, "Cough", spit.

688 ◆ Kiss and tell.

689 ◆ Act like a whore in front of your in-laws.

690 ◆ Ignore your call waiting.

691 ◆ "Borrow" other people's pens and pencils.

692 ◆ Mispronounce a colleague's name – for eleven years.

693 ◆ Leave a few stones unturned.

694 ◆ When your colleague asks if you like his new haircut, cough.

695 ◆ Speed up after you pass the radar.

696 ◆ Pop a child's balloon.

697 ◆ Tell filthy jokes.

698 ◆ Hover aggressively over hors d'oeuvres.

699 ◆ Throw recyclables into the regular trash.

700 ◆ Go ahead: ask what your country can do for you.

701 ◆ Always say never.

702 ◆ Eat ice cream in front of the children and don't share.

703 ◆ Plead poverty.

704 ◆ Leave a long message on your answering machine.

705 ◆ Fall asleep on jury duty.

706 ◆ Ask people how they got their limp.

707 ◆ Fire well before you see the whites of their eyes.

708 ◆ Groan when you sit down.

709 ◆ Groan when you stand up.

710 ◆ Do don't's and don't do do's.

711 ◆ Say "uh-oh" a lot.

712 ◆ Don't give an inch.

713 ◆ Try on underwear in stores.

714 ◆ Name your new baby Rothschild.

715 ◆ Return from the office loo exclaiming: "Boy, that Feen-a-Mint really works."

716 ◆ Examine your Kleenex carefully after use.

717 ◆ Confuse first and second wives.

718 ◆ Leave roller skates on the stairs.

719 ◆ After the first person gives you directions, turn and ask someone else.

720 ◆ If an excuse is good enough to use once, it's good enough to use again.

721 ◆ Ask people to tell you again how their pet died.

722 ◆ In the changing room, stare at people as they undress.

723 ◆ Knock on limousine windows and peer inside.

724 ◆ Tell new neighbours that the neighbourhood's gone downhill.

725 ◆ Dial a wrong number in the middle of the night – twice.

726 ◆ Squeeze your boyfriends' pimples.

727 ◆ A little white lie never hurt anyone.

LIFE'S LITTLE WHITE LIES AND EXCUSES

Knowing how to tell a little lie is integral to getting by in life....

728 ◆ Read my lips.

729 ◆ I'll ask my manager, but I doubt it.

730 ◆ Gee, I guess the invitation was just lost in the mail.

731 ◆ I thought you said you would take care of it.

732 ◆ I'm serious, you look great in that hat.

733 ◆ Have you lost weight?

734 ◆ No problem.

735 ◆ I'll call you.

736 ◆ Take my word for it.

737 ◆ Relax, nothing will go wrong.

738 ◆ Money back guarantee.

739 ◆ I never got the fax.

740 ◆ I'm not angry; I'm not mad.

741 ◆ I'm about to go into a meeting.

742 ◆ The traffic was really bad.

743 ◆ You'll have to pay because I forgot my wallet.

744 ◆ I rarely drink this much.

745 ◆ David's parents said that he could.

746 ◆ I had to go to a funeral.

747 ◆ I'll keep your c.v. on file.

748 ◆ This wrinkle cream actually reverses ageing.

749 ◆ You're too good for me.

750 ◆ This is my last piece of cake.

751 ◆ I'd do it for you.

752 ◆ I'm washing my hair that week.

753 ◆ One adult and four children, please.

754 ◆ Next time it's on me.

755 ◆ I promise not to tell anyone – ever.

756 ◆ My answering machine is broken, and I never got the message.

757 ◆ I was just going to call you.

758 ◆ You can trust me.

759 ◆ This hurts me more than it hurts you.

760 ◆ No offence.

761 ◆ Let me make this perfectly clear.

762 ◆ I am not a crook.

763 ◆ May the best person win.

764 ◆ I'm a size 10.

765 ◆ "All the taste of butter
without the calories."

766 ◆ This is for your own good.

767 ◆ You'll see, this medicine tastes just like cherry syrup.

768 ◆ I never saw him before in my life.

769 ◆ It was the wrong kind of snow.

770 ◆ Honey, I have to work late.

771 ◆ He hit me first.

772 ◆ It was good for me, too.

773 ◆ It's not the money; I love working in the legal profession.

774 ◆ I hear my mother calling me.

775 ◆ Actually, I like the taste of tofu.

776 ◆ It feels so good to be single again.

777 ◆ It's one-of-a-kind.

778 ◆ It's nothing personal, I'm just not interested in dating right now.

779 ◆ It's so simple a child can do it.

780 ◆ I'm really glad you got that off your chest.

781 ◆ I'm just on my way out the door.

782 ◆ My grandmother died. (Again.)

783 ◆ I must be losing my memory.

784 ◆ It's in mint condition.

785 ◆ I knew that.

786 ◆ I never eat. Why am I so fat?

787 ◆ Oh, I thought it was tomorrow night.

788 ◆ This time, I mean it.

789 ♦ You're my favourite
mother-in-law.

790 ◆ I never said that.

791 ◆ I won't make the same mistake again.

792 ◆ I was never told.

793 ◆ You're my best friend in the whole wide world.

794 ◆ I love you.

795 ◆ I love you, too.

796 ◆ If I had to lose, I'm glad you won.

797 ◆ The dog ate my homework.

798 ◆ Please don't take this the wrong way, but....

799 ◆ Sorry, my car broke down.

800 ◆ I didn't feel a thing.

801 ◆ Studies show....

802 ◆ Easy to assemble.

803 ◆ I was only teasing.

804 ◆ I'll be right with you.

805 ◆ We're just good friends.

806 ◆ I followed directions.

807 ◆ I'm not lying. Honest.

808 ◆ That's the cutest baby I've ever seen.

809 ◆ I can't believe that's a toupee – it looks so natural.

810 ◆ I have no idea how this got broken.

811 ◆ I'd love to see more baby pictures.

812 ◆ I'll just go back to sleep for five more minutes.

813 ◆ I'm just smoking to keep my weight down.

814 ◆ I love to have the grandchildren visit.

815 ◆ Honey, that was the best meatloaf I've ever had.

816 ◆ I really only listen to Radio 3.

817 ◆ Back in the old days, I was a handsome devil.

818 ◆ I don't mind sleeping on the floor.

819 ◆ No, I don't mind staying until 9 P.M.

820 ◆ Diet shakes are so satisfying.

821 ◆ I didn't want it, anyway.

822 ◆ I'd love to stay and help, but I have to be somewhere.

823 ◆ Keep driving; I think I know where we are now.

824 ◆ I'd like to still be friends.

825 ◆ It's an honour to meet you, Prime Minister.

826 ◆ What grey hair?

827 ◆ There's a swimsuit to flatter every figure.

828 ◆ My home is your home – stay as long as you like.

829 ◆ I've chosen a bridesmaid dress that you can wear again.

830 ◆ "Handsome, athletic, intelligent,
sensitive, SWM seeks...."

831 ◆ Tastes just like homemade.

832 ◆ ☺ Have a nice day.

LIFE'S LITTLE SELF DESTRUCTIONS

When you're through ragging on everyone else, there's only one person left to torture....

833 ◆ Apologize even if you didn't do anything.

834 ◆ Apologize for living.

835 ◆ Apologize for apologizing.

836 ◆ Live in a constant state of denial.

837 ◆ Don't fasten your seat belt – you're only going for a quick drive.

838 ◆ Forget to sign your Christmas cards.

839 ◆ Lock your keys in the car.

840 ◆ Monopolize the most boring person at a dinner party.

841 ◆ Step off the kerb without checking for puddles.

842 ◆ Buy a budgerigar for your cat.

843 ◆ As you introduce your husband, forget his name.

844 ◆ Shoot a whole roll without any film.

845 ◆ Break a mirror.

846 ◆ Stand on rickety old chairs.

847 ◆ Need to be in two places at once.

848 ◆ Tell your friends to drop by your summer home any weekend.

849 ◆ Leap before you look.

850 ◆ Change your mind.

851 ◆ Change it back.

852 ◆ Delay until it's too late.

853 ◆ Write a nasty letter to the Inland Revenue.

854 ◆ Bawl out a policeman while he's writing you a ticket.

855 ◆ Suggest meeting your blind date at a top-less bar.

856 ◆ Describe your sex life to your in-laws.

857 ◆ If something goes wrong, eat a whole bag of potato chips.

858 ◆ If you go up to the limit on your credit card, get another one.

859 ◆ Bite your nails while you are waiting.

860 ◆ If at first you don't succeed, cry.

861 ◆ If you don't come from a dysfunctional family, make one up.

862 ◆ Unload your problems on your kids.

863 ◆ Compare yourself to others for that greater than/less than feeling.

864 ◆ List your membership in AA on your c.v.

865 ◆ Start that long drive home when you're drowsy.

866 ◆ When the relationship is definitely over, try to make it work again.

867 ◆ When he cheats on you, make it up to him.

868 ◆ See an ineffectual psychiatrist for years.

869 ◆ Support your friend's coke habit.

870 ◆ Hide the bottle in plain sight.

871 ◆ Let every stranger control your life.

872 ◆ Say yes when you mean no.

873 ◆ Buy yet another diet book.

874 ◆ If you're not the oppressor, be the victim.

875 ◆ Work for your ex.

876 ◆ Spend all your holidays
with your parents.

877 ◆ Be a wallflower.

878 ◆ Walk with your eyes down.

879 ◆ Nap during your therapy session.

880 ◆ Always let people go ahead of you in the queue.

881 ◆ Wake up and smell the manure.

882 ◆ Rationalize away your problems.

883 ◆ Make up your mind and don't change.

884 ◆ Never look people in the eye.

885 ◆ Wear white when you have your period.

886 ◆ At the Bingo hall buy a vowel that's been called already.

887 ◆ Spend more than you earn.

888 ◆ Agree with everyone else all the time.

889 ◆ Make important decisions by flipping a coin.

890 ◆ Tell different lies to different people until you forget what the truth is.

891 ◆ Tell people you're recovering.

892 ◆ Only see one solution.

893 ◆ Ask people who don't like you for help.

894 ◆ Don't feel your feelings.

895 ◆ Heave a sigh and do what they want
anyway.

896 ◆ Be assertive ... NOT!

897 ◆ Always mount a horse on its right side.

898 ◆ Pull on an itchy label and rip the collar.

899 ◆ The night before your big job interview, set your alarm clock for 6:00 P.M.

900 ◆ Buy expensive things on impulse.

901 ◆ Sit directly down on the public toilet seat without looking first.

902 ◆ If you're ever lucky enough to meet the Queen, give her a big hug.

903 ◆ Order pesto fettucini with lobster at a job interview lunch.

904 ◆ Forget your passport.

905 ◆ After the second date, move in together.

906 ◆ Wear pastel blue leisure suits and white loafers.

907 ◆ Pack heavy groceries into flimsy bags.

908 ◆ Enter a beauty pageant.

909 ◆ Let life pass you by.

910 ◆ Ignore expiry dates on prescription bottles.

911 ◆ Blame yourself for everyone else's problems.

912 ◆ Turn off your computer before saving your work.

913 ◆ Load up on goodies for "unexpected company".

914 ◆ Tape a stupid TV show over your all-time favourite movie.

915 ◆ Machine wash your silk dress.

916 ◆ Invite your mother-in-law for a visit when your mother is already ensconced in the guest room.

917 ◆ Sit next to the fattest person on a long distance coach journey.

918 ◆ Believe him when he says his wife doesn't understand him.

919 ◆ Flush your diamond engagement ring down the toilet to prove you're angry with him.

920 ◆ Save that snapshot that makes you look like a cow.

921 ◆ Call him every ten minutes.

922 ◆ Send an expensive wedding gift but forget to include your name.

923 ◆ Leave your sex toys around when the cleaning lady comes.

924 ◆ Bring your talkative friend along to a silent retreat.

925 ◆ Try a complicated new recipe for your last-minute dinner party.

926 ◆ Call in sick and then go lunch-time shopping right near your office.

927 ◆ Just for a change, walk home down the dark, narrow alley.

928 ◆ Jump in the shower with no towel in sight.

929 ◆ Order a diet cola with a huge scoop of ice cream.

930 ◆ So you're allergic, eat it anyway.

931 ◆ Lend your friend money just one more time.

932 ◆ Arrive at the airport five minutes before your international flight.

933 ◆ Ask a chronic complainer, "How are you?"

934 ◆ Rent the flat over a night club.

935 ◆ Decide to attend a college you've never visited.

936 ◆ Flaunt your infidelity.

937 ◆ Forget to check the petrol gauge.

938 ◆ Forget to lock the toilet door.

939 ◆ Add chlorine bleach to the coloured wash.

940 ◆ Attempt to break up a fight on the Underground.

941 ◆ Buy running shoes without trying them on.

942 ◆ Sit home on a Saturday night and wait for his call.

943 ◆ Clean your loaded handgun.

944 ◆ In front of the children.

945 ◆ Assume the bank NEVER makes a mistake.

946 ◆ Keep your money under your mattress.

947 ◆ Be the designated driver when drinks are on the house.

948 ◆ Enjoy a huge meal before you ride the roller coaster.

949 ◆ Call 0898 numbers and talk for hours.

950 ◆ Threaten your kids with, "Wait until Daddy gets home."

951 ◆ Let your make-up dry out – especially blue eyeshadow.

952 ◆ Belabour a point.

953 ◆ Belabour a point.

954 ◆ Talk too fast.

955 ◆ Don't pay your bookie.

956 ◆ Kiss a frog and hope it becomes a prince.

957 ◆ Talk only about yourself on a first date.

958 ◆ Drink the water in Mexico.

959 ◆ Drink the contents of your finger bowl at a formal state dinner.

960 ◆ Get dressed in the dark.

961 ◆ Just say "Yes."

962 ◆ Ask to see more wedding pictures.

963 ◆ Eat more fried foods.

964 ◆ Pick your teeth with the business card a client has just handed you.

965 ◆ Pay extra for the one-hour dry-cleaning service and come back three weeks later to pick it up.

966 ◆ Ask your lawyer to contact the jurors to improve the odds of winning your case.

967 ◆ Volunteer to be the "before" model in diet ads.

968 ◆ Don't name your computer files.

969 ◆ Choose your career on the advice of a psychic.

970 ◆ Correct your boss in front of his peers.

971 ◆ Let the toddlers have as much chocolate as they want.

972 ◆ Post important letters without a stamp.

973 ◆ Volunteer your house for the wedding reception.

974 ◆ Obsess over a celebrity.

975 ◆ Drink coffee close to bedtime.

976 ◆ Tear up a photo of the Pope on national television.

977 ◆ Binge and purge.

978 ◆ Look for true love in the personal ads.

979 ◆ Tuck your skirt into your tights after going to the loo.

980 ◆ Make a pass at your sister's husband.

981 ◆ Joke about shooting the Queen while queuing for the Buck House tour.

982 ◆ Rely on your memory.

983 ◆ Load up on prunes before a hot date.

984 ◆ Stick the bubbling hot pizza right in your mouth.

985 ◆ Plead ignorance.

986 ◆ Walk under a ladder.

987 ◆ Stop using four-letter words and try labels like cretin, doofus, and schmuck.

988 ◆ Get a job making cold calls at meal times.

989 ◆ Over-react.

990 ◆ Wear tights that sag.

991 ◆ Be co-dependent.

992 ◆ Make promises you can't possibly keep.

993 ◆ Miss two hire purchase payments.

994 ◆ Toilet train her before she's ready.

995 ◆ Pick up the bill all the time.

996 ◆ Play with fire.

997 ◆ When he asks for all the details, tell him.

998 ◆ Ask for trouble.

999 ◆ Play hard to get when you want to get got.

1000 ◆ Bake like a flounder in the hot summer sun.

1001 ◆ Hang your handbag over the back of your chair in crowded restaurants.

1002 ◆ Put the wrong letters in the wrong envelopes.

1003 ◆ Play with your vegetables.

1004 ◆ Cut in front of London taxis.

1005 ◆ Whenever your child whines for a new toy, buy it.

1006 ◆ Leave the tube of black shoe polish near the toothpaste.

1007 ◆ Look on the dark side.

1008 ◆ Cross your fingers when you tell a lie.

1009 ◆ Ward off evil spirits with garlic.

1010 ◆ Let people wipe their feet on you.

1011 ◆ Have the foggiest idea.

1012 ◆ Step out on the ledge to wash the high-rise windows.

1013 ◆ Don't do today what you can put off until tomorrow.

1014 ◆ Press your luck.

1015 ◆ Skate on thin ice.

1016 ◆ Judge a book by its cover.

1017 ◆ Don't replace the spare.

1018 ◆ Open mouth. Insert foot.

1019 ◆ Wear diamonds, gold necklaces, and furs on the Underground.

1020 ◆ Try to please all of the people all of the time.

1021 ◆ Seek out negative influences.

1022 ◆ Believe everything you read.

1023 ◆ Mull it over in the middle of the night.

1024 ◆ Vote Conservative.

1025 ◆ Break up; go back; break up; go back.

1026 ◆ Go to work with a little cotton wool on your chin.

1027 ◆ Keep imagining everything else that can go wrong.

1028 ◆ Ask for a haircut when you want a trim.

1029 ◆ Insist on having the last word.